Children of the
ECUADOREAN HIGHLANDS

THE WORLD'S CHILDREN

Children of the
ECUADOREAN
HIGHLANDS

BARBARA BEIRNE

🌸 Carolrhoda Books, Inc./Minneapolis

I would like to thank my son Christopher, a great traveling companion, for sharing his apartment in Quito.

Special thanks to Patrick McGeehan, Sara McDaniels, Maria Zimmerman, the Lopez family, and the Andes Manta folk music group.

Carolrhoda Books, Inc. c/o The Lerner Group
241 First Avenue North, Minneapolis, MN 55401

LIBRARY OF CONGRESS CATALOGING-IN-PUBLICATION DATA

Beirne, Barbara.
  Children of the Eucadorean highlands / Barbara Beirne.
    p. cm. — (The world's children)
Includes index.
  Summary: An introduction to the history, geography and culture of Ecuador's mountain areas, with a focus on the day-to-day lives of the children.
  ISBN 1–57505–000–5
  1. Sierra (Ecuador)—Social life and customs—Juvenile literature.
2. Children—Ecuador—Sierra—Social life and customs—Juvenile literature. [1. Ecuador—Social life and customs.] I. Title. II. Series: World's children (Minneapolis, Minn.)
F3741.A6B45 1996   95–45251

Manufactured in the United States of America
1 2 3 4 5 6 – JR – 01 00 99 98 97 96

Each morning when Maria wakes up, she pulls on her red wool poncho and places her felt hat on her head. The people in Maria's community always wear warm clothing because they live high in the mountains. Maria lives in Ecuador, a country in South America, right on the equator.

The word *ecuador* actually means "equator" in Spanish. The equator is an imaginary line that divides the earth into equal halves—the north half and the south half. Because the sun shines down close to the equator throughout the year, temperatures in Ecuador stay about the same all year long. The temperature depends on the altitude rather than the seasons. In Ecuador's mountain areas, where Maria lives, it can be like spring in the valley while the mountain peaks are covered by snow and ice.

Since the temperature does not change much throughout the year, seasons in Ecuador tend to be wet or dry rather than hot or cold. Summer, or the dry season, runs from about June through October, and winter, or the rainy season, extends from November through May.

This marker sits at the side of a road that crosses the equator. It shows travelers where the imaginary line of the equator divides the earth into north and south.

7

Ecuador, located in the northwest corner of South America, is about the size of the state of Colorado. The Andes Mountains stretch down the middle of Ecuador, from its northern border with Colombia to its southern neighbor, Peru.

There are two separate Andean mountain chains. The western mountain chain is called Cordillera Occidental, and the eastern chain is called Cordillera Oriental. The two mountain ranges are connected by strips of high flatland that span the valley between the mountains like rungs on a ladder. This mountainous area is called the Sierra or the highlands. Almost half of Ecuador's people live in the highlands.

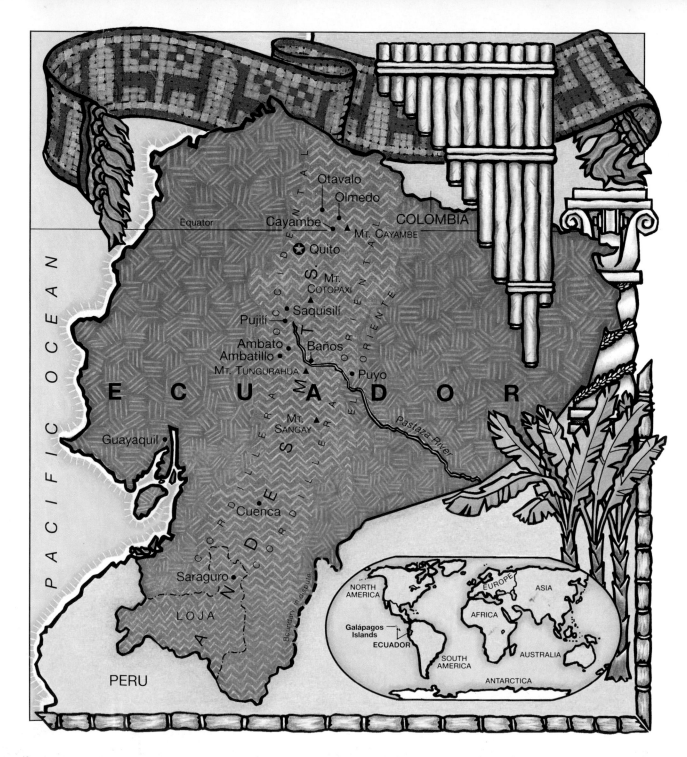

Maria lives in a village on the slopes of Mount Cayambe in the Oriental range. The village is over a mile above sea level. Maria's family raises potatoes to eat and a few sheep for wool. Maria helps by watching over the animals and bringing in the vegetables. She has never been to a city. Her ancestors have lived here for hundreds if not thousands of years.

It is believed that the first settlements in this area started over 12,000 years ago. Because the mountains made traveling difficult, each isolated village developed its own customs and traditions.

In the 15th century, the Incas, a powerful nation from the area now known as Peru, sent armies to what is now Ecuador and little by little conquered the entire highland area. The Incas built roads and planted new crops. They insisted that everyone in the highlands speak the Incan language— Quechua.

Even so, many highland villagers worked to keep their languages and traditions as much as they could. That's why the people of Maria's village still have many customs and words that are older than the Incas and different from some others in the Sierra. There are also differences in the traditional dress of the peoples in the highlands.

Maria's village in the mountains

Quito, with its tall buildings, is the home of the Palacio de Gobierno—the building where Ecuador's democratically elected president lives and works.

The Incas formed a government center in Quito, which is the capital of Ecuador today. Quito does not look the way it did when the Incan emperors ruled, because the Spaniards came searching for gold less than one hundred years after the Incas' arrival. The Incas, with their spears and arrows, were no match for the horses and cannons of the Spanish conquistadors. When the Incas realized defeat was near, they burned down Quito rather than surrender it.

Pedro lives in an apartment building in Quito. His parents, like many other highlanders, moved from their farm in the mountains to the city with hopes of earning more money. Pedro often helps his mother after school. They sell chili peppers, oranges, and shoes on the street.

Pedro likes selling in the Plaza San Francisco. It has a huge fountain and is busy with tourists walking about and street vendors selling things. There is a beautiful church on the plaza named for Quito's patron saint, San Francisco. The church, built by the Spanish conquerors, is one of the oldest buildings in Quito.

Left and below: *Plaza San Francisco*

Lupita and Joanne also live in Quito. They are nine years old and are in their fourth year at a primary school.

The girls and their relatives, along with most of the population of Ecuador, are mestizos. This Spanish word for "mixed" means that Joanne's and Lupita's ancestors are both Spanish and Indian. Maria and Pedro are considered Indians because their ancestors lived here before the Spanish.

Joanne's parents own a restaurant on a busy street in Quito. The specialty of the restaurant is *cebiche,* which is fish or shrimp with a sauce made of orange juice, tomatoes, onions, and chili peppers. The seafood is trucked or flown in from Ecuador's coast.

While waiting for her parents to finish working, Joanne plays *rayuela* with her friends. This game is similar to hopscotch.

Since Joanne's family lives above the restaurant, she can sit by her bedroom window and look out at the beautiful city's many buildings made with tile roofs, white-ash walls, and wooden doors. In the distance, she can see Panecillo Hill. Sometimes on a clear day, she can

Joanne and her friends play rayuela.

see the snow-capped volcano, Cotopaxi.

There are at least thirty volcanic peaks in Ecuador's highlands, an area once called "The Avenue of Volcanoes" by an explorer. Some of the volcanoes are extinct, but at least eight are smoldering. The last volcano to erupt was Mount Sangay in 1946.

Mount Cotopaxi

Panecillo Hill in Quito.

15

Roberto is eleven years old and is of mostly Spanish heritage. He attends a private school and hopes to go to one of Quito's universities someday. He is in sixth grade, the last grade in primary school.

In class, Roberto's teacher uses the newspaper to get students to talk about world events. Roberto and his classmates are eager to tell her what they've heard on the radio and TV. They usually speak in Spanish, but sometimes they practice their English.

After class, Roberto sometimes makes plans with his friends to go to the Avenida de las Amazonas on the weekend. Here they can visit a music shop and listen to some of the latest rock music from the United States, Europe, and Latin America. They might also buy a pizza or go to a movie.

Below: *Roberto raises his hand to answer a question in class.* Below left: *In most schools, the students wear uniforms. For many children, their uniforms are their best outfits and are sometimes worn for important occasions.*

Most highland students do not go on to a university. Some set up their own businesses or go to training schools to learn useful skills.

Julia, who is seventeen, is learning to can vegetables. Tayo and Juan are learning to sew together leather dress shoes.

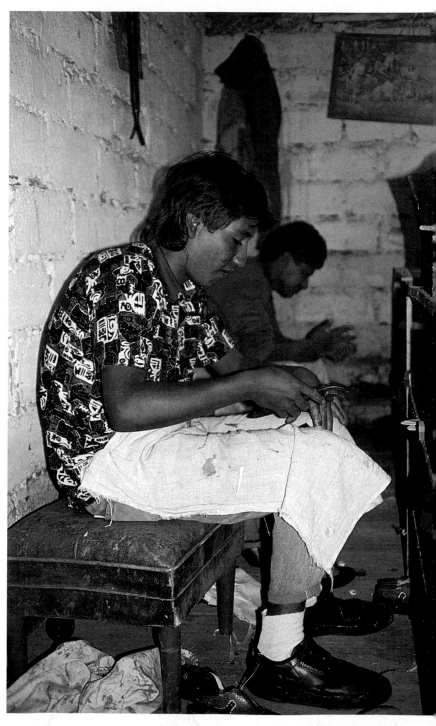

Bernadette lives in a town called Otavalo, about seventy miles northwest of Quito. In Otavalo, expert weavers make wall hangings, ponchos, belts, pocketbooks, and other colorful woven items. Weavers first shear the wool from the sheep. Then they spin the wool and color it with vegetable dyes before weaving it.

For generations, weavers have used wooden looms, passing down their weaving techniques from the grandparents and parents to the children.

Bernadette (left) *sells her family's woven goods* (below).

Rosario, Bernadette's sister, is working hard at her mother's loom to get the family pattern right. She wants her poncho to look better than the ponchos being made at small factories that produce items made of artificial fibers and dyes.

Woven items made by hand and made in factories are sold at Otavalo's Saturday market—one of the largest in the country. Tourists come from around the country and the world to buy Otavalo's woven goods. Some people from Otavalo also travel across the globe to sell their products.

Above: *Rosario (on right) works at the loom with her cousin's help.*

19

Bernadette and Rosario's young cousin

This weekend will be an exciting one for Bernadette and Rosario. They have a new little cousin, and the women in their family have spent many hours helping their aunt care for the new baby. Everyone is looking forward to the baby's Catholic christening. Although some Ecuadoreans still practice ancient relgions, most are Roman Catholic, a religion introduced to them by the Spanish.

On the day of the christening, everyone will wear his or her finest clothes. The men of Otavalo wear dark blue ponchos and white cotton pants. The women wear beautiful embroidered blouses with long skirts. The people of Otavalo are very proud of their heritage.

The women of Bernadette and Rosario's family outside the church

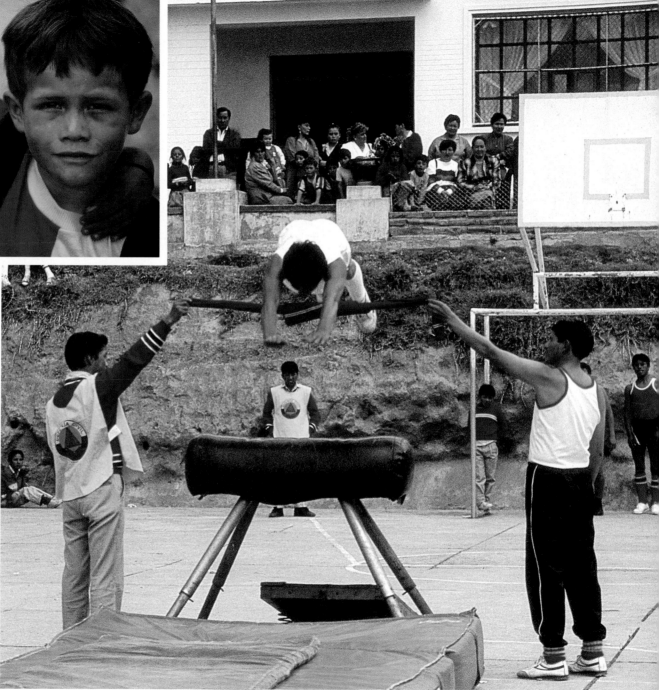

In Pujillí, a village a couple hours south of Quito, the whole community has gathered at the school to watch a gymnastic exhibition. This is a big event, where professionals as well as students perform.

Juan and Pablo proudly wear their gymnastic uniforms. The boys also use their uniforms for their favorite sport—*fútbol* (called soccer in the United States). Fútbol is the favorite sport of most boys their age. Juan and Pablo would like to get so good at the game that they could be part of the Ecuadorean national team and play in the World Cup someday.

21

After working hard all day on his reading, math, and science, José (below right) *likes to swing on the parallel bars with his classmates (below). They also play* canicas— *a game similar to marbles that is sometimes played with small coins* (right).

José lives in Ambatillo, a village in the highlands near the city of Ambato in the central Sierra. Even though it takes over an hour to walk to school, José loves going. Before 1970, all the classes in Ecuador were taught in Spanish. Now José's teacher speaks Quechua, since this is spoken by many people in the highlands.

José's family has a farm and one pig. After school, José hoes the soil around the corn and quinoa. Quinoa is a tiny, round grain that looks like a seed. Quinoa is often boiled in water and eaten for lunch or dinner. Sometimes José's mother mixes quinoa with potatoes, meat, or cheese.

Occasionally on Saturdays when José does not have chores, he climbs the hills behind his home to visit his friend Carlos. As José climbs, the weather becomes cooler and the air becomes thinner. José doesn't notice. His body is used to the high altitude.

On this trip, José happens to meet a young man and his mother. The woman carries a spindle and wool. She takes a piece of the wool sheared from a sheep, and as she walks, twists the wool between her fingers into thread. José knows children as young as five years old who can spin wool into thread.

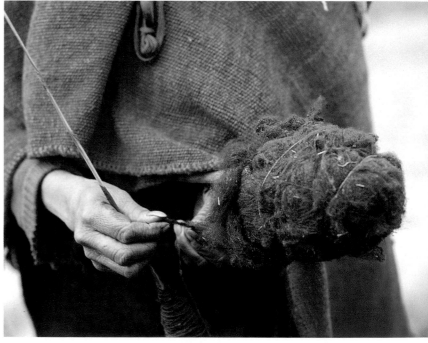

Above: *Twisting wool into thread*

José finally sees the curve of the dirt street where Carlos lives. Carlos and his sister, Irene, rush to greet him. They are happy to have a visitor, and they spend the afternoon playing *fútbol* with a ball made of yarn.

Carlos and his family live in a one-room hut with a dirt floor and thatched roof. The hut does not have a bathroom or electricity. The family uses candles for light at night. Carlos's father is a farmer, but he is too poor to own the land. The owner of the land lets the family live on it without paying rent. The Ecuadorean government is trying to help people come to legally own the land they live on.

Left: *Irene and Carlos.* Above: *Carlos and Irene's father comes out to greet José. Their mother stands in the doorway of their hut with their baby brother.*

Not far from the farm where Carlos and his family live is a large plantation with many fields, called a hacienda. Haciendas are usually owned by rich Ecuadoreans of mostly Spanish descent. The manager of the hacienda often hires extra people to help plant the corn or till the soil. When work is available, José's father and Carlos's father both work there. The money they earn helps their families buy a few chickens or guinea pigs. In Ecuador, people raise guinea pigs to eat. They are called *cuy* because they squeal *cuy, cuy, cuy.*

While their fathers are away, the boys stay home from school to help on the family farm. In Ecuador, children must attend school between the ages of six and fourteen. It is not unusual, though, for students to be absent when their family needs help on their farm.

Manuel and his family are also farmers. They own a small farm where they grow sugarcane. Most of Ecuador's sugarcane is grown on the coast where there are large plantations, but Manuel's farm is near Baños in the center of the Sierra. After school, Manuel goes to the town square where he sells sugarcane. He also sells raw brown-sugar cakes, which are a popular treat in the highlands.

Many tourists come to Baños, a popular health resort, to enjoy the hot baths. They also come for the warm, comfortable climate and views of the volcano, Tungurahua. The visitors stop at Manuel's stall as they stroll through town.

Above: *Manuel holding sugarcane at his family's stand.* Left: *Brightly colored buildings in Baños*

Sometimes Manuel and his family sell their sugarcane products in Puyo, a small town a few hours drive by bus from Baños. Puyo is on the eastern edge of the highlands.

As they drive to Puyo, Manuel watches the landscape change. During the first part of their journey, the narrow road takes them up and down the mountainside with its view of the Pastaza River. Later it becomes hot and humid, and the view disappears as a mist blankets the land.

Left: *The four-hundred-mile-long Pastaza River begins in the highlands.*
Below: *The road to Puyo*

During the rainy season, umbrellas are very important for the children of Puyo.

Puyo is known as the gateway to Ecuador's jungle, which makes up about 45 percent of Ecuador's land. In the jungle, known in Ecuador as the Oriente region, there are thick rain forests and many rivers formed from melted snow. Trees, vines, flowers, and other plants grow so close together in these rain forests that it is difficult to cut a way through them.

Some people from the highlands have moved to the Oriente. They try to start farms on sections of rain forest that have been cleared.

Others find jobs in the oil fields there.

Puyo has always been a popular stopping place for traders, missionaries, and travelers before they venture into the jungle. There are many stores in Puyo to provide food and supplies.

A street at the edge of Puyo

A boy and his mother shop for corn, while a baby rests comfortably by the pile.

Left: *A busy day at the market in Saquisilí.* Below: Llapingachos, *a popular food in Ecuador made with potatoes and cheese, are sold at the market. Llapingachos are sometimes eaten as a main dish, and they are often served with a sauce.*

In other areas of the highlands, there are few stores. People depend on the weekly markets to provide for their needs. One of the most popular markets besides the one in Otavalo is in Saquisilí, a town in the central highlands.

On Thursday mornings, people seem to come to Saquisilí from all directions. Some come by bus or truck, but most walk, carrying vegetables they have grown or treasures they have decided to sell or trade.

Anita usually helps her family by tending the sheep before and after school. But today she is bringing the sheep to market. She hurries because she doesn't want to miss anything. Perhaps a few sheep will be sold, and her family will be able to buy treats, such as smoked cod, trucked in from Ecuador's coast. They might also buy some pork to add to the locro, *a milk-and-potato soup Anita's mother makes.*

Another important market is in Cuenca, a Spanish colonial city founded in 1557. Cuenca is in the southern highlands and is the third largest city in Ecuador. Only Quito and Guayaquil, a seaport on the coast, are larger.

Cuenca is home to the Panama hat industry. The hats are made of raw *toquilla*—a flexible, fine straw that comes from a palmlike tree that grows on the coast. The *toquilla* is trucked in to Cuenca.

Adults and children alike weave *toquilla* into hats in their homes, on the streets, or in the fields while watching cattle. The hats are left untrimmed and then sold at the market in Cuenca to hat dealers who take them to a factory to be trimmed, bleached, and shaped.

Panama hats were never made in Panama. They received their name from the many travelers to Panama who purchased the Ecuadorean straw hats while traveling through the Isthmus of Panama or working on the Panama Canal.

South of Cuenca is the Loja Province, a rugged area that borders Peru. There are no volcanoes in this part of Ecuador. People raise some cattle and barley and use oxen to plow their fields.

In the town of Saraguro, the majority of the population is mestizo. A small native group called the Saraguros live in this area. They are direct descendants of the Incas, and their families have lived here since the middle of the 15th century.

It is believed that Tupac Yupanqui, the Inca conqueror, brought Saraguros to Ecuador from their homes in Peru because they were loyal to him. He sent the villagers who originally lived in this area to Bolivia.

Opposite page and right: *Saraguros wearing traditional black or indigo-blue wool clothing. Some say black is worn by the Saraguros in mourning for the death of Atahualpa, the last Incan emperor. Others believe black is worn to express longing for their Peruvian homeland.*

Few events are more exciting or colorful than Ecuadorean festivals. Many of the masks are made of papier-mâché and cloth.

Long before the Incas conquered the highlands, villagers held dramatic celebrations to thank the gods for their favors. After Spanish missionaries brought Roman Catholicism to the highlands, these new Christian beliefs often combined with old religious beliefs, and the festivals continued. For example, the Inca harvest holiday of Inti-Raymi, usually held in June, is now celebrated as part of the Catholic holy day of Corpus Christi.

Every year in Olmedo, a village in the northern highlands near the town of Cayambe, there is a festival to celebrate the traditions of this five-hundred-year-old village. A parade and fiesta are held to remind the community of their ancestors and to help the children understand their heritage.

It takes months of preparation for the villagers to make all the costumes and masks for the celebration. Scary masks are the most popular. They are worn to frighten away evil spirits.

Juanita and Esperanza dress up for the festival in jewelry that has been passed down in their families. Their blouses, belts, and skirts are similar to those their ancestors wore long ago.

Though excited about the parade, the girls are nervous about the crowds. They stay together, close to their parents.

This year Dolores gets to ride in the parade. Her father was chosen to be the *prioste*. A *prioste* is the host of the festival. The person selected is usually an important member of the community. It is such a great honor to be selected that no one ever refuses, even though the *prioste* pays all of the festival expenses.

Juanita and Esperanza

Dolores and the village women have brushed and decorated her llama especially for the parade. Llamas are important to the people of the Sierra. Highlanders use llama wool for clothes, hides for sandals, and dung for fuel.

Llamas are best known as pack animals. Llamas can carry packs for days without food or water. Of course, if a llama is asked to carry something too heavy, it will refuse. In fact, the llama will sit on the ground and refuse to move until its load is made lighter. Dolores is just the right size.

Left and below: *Dolores rides her llama in the Olmedo parade. It is said that llamas lived in the highlands 2,000 years before the Incas arrived.*

While the parade dances forward, music can be heard everywhere. Panpipes and flutes, made from the staff of the bamboo plant, are the most popular instruments.

It is a tradition in most of the highland villages for only the men to play instruments. The women join in by singing and dancing. The songs have a rhythm that is repeated over and over. This repetition in the music is part of tradition in the Andes.

Above: *The panpipe, called a* rondador, *was invented in Ecuador centuries ago. It is made with numerous pipes of different thicknesses and lengths. Each piece of bamboo has to be perfect, and each pipe must be carefully tuned. Luis Lopez took three months to make his* rondador.

Right: *Stringed instruments, along with the accordion and saxophone, were introduced by the Spanish and are still widely used.*

Boys shake an instrument made of goat toenails while the other musicians play.

A rodeo, with a calf-roping contest, is also a tradition here. The children wait eagerly to watch this event, even though they know the calves will be set free the next day.

By dusk, the people of Olmedo are tired, but they pull their ponchos closer around them and stay as long as they can. As the children go to bed, they can still hear the wonderful music and feel a pride in their highland traditions that warms their hearts as they drift off to sleep.

Pronunciation Guide

canicas: kah-NEE-kus
cebiche: say-BEE-chay
Cordillera Occidental: kor-dee-YEH-rah
  ohk-see-den-TAHL
Cordillera Oriental: kor-dee-YEH-rah
  oh-ree-en-TAHL
Oriente: oh-ree-EN-tay
Inti-Raymi: in-tee-RAHY-mee
fútbol: FUHT-bohl
hacienda: ah-see-EN-dah
llapingachos: yah-pin-GAH-chohs
locro: LOH-krow
mestizo: mes-TEE-zoh
prioste: pree-OHS-tay
Quechua: KETCH-wah
rayuela: rah-oo-WEH-lah
quinoa: KEEN-wah
rondador: rohn-dah-DOHR
toquilla: toh-KEE-yah

Index

Photo Credits:
Additional photos courtesy of: Elaine Little, pp. 16 (both), 17 (both), 19 (right), 21 (both); Sara McDaniels, pp. 10, 12 (both), 35 (both), 36, 37; Dr. Ellen Ordway, p. 15 (right).